FAMILY VIOLENCE

Debra Goldentyer

Austin, Texas

© Copyright 1995 Steck-Vaughn Co.

All rights reserved. No part of this book may be reproduced or utilized in any form or by any means, electronic or mechanical, including photocopying, recording, or by any information storage and retrieval system, without permission in writing from the Publisher. Inquiries should be addressed to:
   Steck-Vaughn Company, P.O. Box 26015, Austin, TX 78755

Consultants:
Beverly Arneth, Director, Family Guidance Center, Trenton, NJ
William B. Presnell, American Association for Marriage and Family Therapy

Developed for Steck-Vaughn Company by Visual Education Corporation, Princeton, New Jersey
Project Director: Paula McGuire
Editors: Jewel Moulthrop, Linda Perrin
Photo Research: Sara Matthews

Raintree Steck-Vaughn Publishers staff
Editor: Kathy Presnell
Project Manager: Julie Klaus
Electronic Production: Scott Melcer
Photo Editor: Margie Foster

Library of Congress Cataloging-in-Publication Data
Goldentyer, Debra, 1960-
    Family violence / Debra Goldentyer.
       p.   cm. — (Teen hot line)
    Includes index.
    ISBN 0-8114-3816-3
    1. Family violence — United States — Juvenile literature. 2. Child abuse — United States — Juvenile literature. [1. Family violence. 2. Child abuse.]
    I. Title. II. Series.
    HQ809.3.U5G64   1995
    306.87 — dc20   94-29680
                                                                                      CIP
                                                                                      AC

Photo Credits: Cover: © Park Street; **15** © James L. Schaffer/PhotoEdit; **17** © Bill Aron/PhotoEdit; **20** © Robert Brenner/PhotoEdit; **25** © Mary Kate Denny/PhotoEdit; **29** © Tony Freeman/PhotoEdit; **32** © Robert Brenner/PhotoEdit; **39** © Myrlene Ferguson/PhotoEdit; **46** © Michael Newman/PhotoEdit; **49** © Bill Aron/PhotoEdit; **54** © Comstock; © **62** Robert Brenner/PhotoEdit; **71** © Richard Hutchings/PhotoEdit; **73** © Shirley Zeiberg; **74** © Mary Kate Denny/PhotoEdit.

Printed and bound in the United States

1 2 3 4 5 6 7 8 9 0 LB 99 98 97 96 95

What the Teen Hot Line Is All About 4
Interview 6
Bulletin Board 10
Chapter 1: Communicating 12
Chapter 2: Families and Violence 19
Chapter 3: The Causes of Violence 28
Chapter 4: Sexual Abuse—A Form of Violence 37
Chapter 5: Doing Something About It 48
Chapter 6: What Happens When You Tell 56
Interview 64
Chapter 7: Righting the Wrongs 69
Where to Go for Help 76
For More Information 77
Index 79

What the Teen Hot Line Is All About

This book is like a telephone hot line. It answers questions about family violence that may be worrying you. Answering these questions requires us to give you the facts. You can use these facts to make your own decisions about what you're going to do about the abuse and violence you may be suffering or may know someone else is suffering. So think of us as the voice on the phone, always there to answer your questions, even the ones that are hard to ask.

Just so you know where we stand, we have made a list of steps that we think everybody should take when they find themselves in any violent or abusive situation. These steps are based on using common sense and protecting yourself, and they assume that you want to do what's best for you.

1. Read books and call hot lines to find out what you need to know about violence and abuse.

2 Talk to others you trust—friends, teachers, parents, and other adults—about what you're going through.

3 Think about what's happening to you and what you want to do about it.

4 Decide whether or not you want to report the abuse, and if you decide to do so, report it.

5 Stick with your decision—if you report the situation, follow up by doing what the authorities tell you to do.

6 Whether you report the situation or not, take care of yourself by asking for protection if you need it and by getting counseling or joining support groups for people who have problems like yours.

We hope that after you read this book you will have the answers to your questions and perhaps to some you hadn't thought of yet. At the back of this book is a list of sources for further information. By thinking about the issues raised in this book you will have made an important effort in taking control of your life.

Interview

Len grew up in what he thought was an average suburban family. He didn't know whether it was average or not; he did know, however, that he got beaten regularly by his father. While no one person's story can be considered typical, Len's story does illustrate many of the problems facing people who grow up in a violent household.

I got hit a lot, really often. Several times a week, I'm pretty sure. I don't know how much of it I remember.

It was unpredictable. There's this idea that you do something that's right, and you're rewarded, and you do something wrong, and you're punished. There's a connection between what happens to you, physically or emotionally, and what you've done.

In my house, it didn't work that way. My father struck back in a way that didn't seem connected to my actions. The same thing often happens in alcoholic families (which mine wasn't) — the abuse is more of a function of who's drunk and who's not and less a function of what the child has done or not done.

If you're young, you have to assume that if they're hitting you, they're the authority, they must be right; you must have done something wrong. I don't think I could have thought that it was his problem.

It wasn't just the physical abuse. He'd do other things.

Whenever we'd go drive into the city to visit my mother's parents, we could never just go; there'd always be a scene. We'd be waiting in the car; then he'd decide he wasn't going to go, and he'd go storming into the house, and my sister or I would be sent to plead, and this would go on for an hour or two, every time. And it was a way of terrorizing the family. And it was, I'm sure, deliberate on a certain level, forcing himself to be the center of everything.

When I was hit, my mother was always in a difficult situation; she didn't want to see it happen, but if she tried to intervene too much, he would really turn on her. I don't know if he ever hit her, but he was very good at making her miserable.

A lot of times, she'd plead with him to stop, but more often, she'd just not want to deal with it. If she tried to comfort me, he'd yell at her for that. My mother's parents always tried to step in. They thought it was outrageous that he hit me. He just ignored them. He said, "My decision, my control. Get out."

I knew how to get at him, too, I guess: tease him about things—about being fat, about smoking. Sure, I knew I'd get hit, but because I couldn't get love, I did it to get attention, OK? And that was the closest I got, so I probably deliberately did things wrong.

I don't know why he did it, what frustrations he had; he was a frustrated, bitter man. How much of it he saw, I can't say. I was never able to get him to talk about it, even much later as an adult. I mean, I sort of tried, and then I realized at some point that I didn't have the right to do that. It wasn't my business, ultimately, which sort of surprised me to realize, but it was his task, not mine.

I hit him back once; I punched him in the chest. Two years later, I found out I'd broken his ribs. I had no idea; I didn't hit him hard at all. At the time I guess something clicked in him, and he wanted to protect me. So he never told me.

It didn't occur to me until years later that his behavior was really perverse. Parents set the tone; they define a world for you. When you're growing up, you don't know if you're rich or poor because you can't tell that until you go look at your neighbor. It's the same thing; you know, there's no outside standard or framework that provides a comparison and enables a child to say, "This isn't reasonable."

It was more the psychological terror than the physical. I could take being hit; I didn't like it, but, you know, being hit isn't the hard part, it's being hit by someone who's supposed to love you.

It still has an effect on me. In relationships, I can feel rejected or abandoned very easily. And, you know, I can see it and almost even control it, but sometimes I can't. I mean, I look at it and think, "You're reacting in a way that's really not warranted in this situation. You're playing out something else." And then I think, "Yeah. Can you do something about it? I don't think so."

I see families sometimes now, and I think, "Oh, they're really nice and relaxed and cool and all that," and other times I see a family and think, "Yeah, they're just like the suburban, violent, stupid, stubborn family I came from."

I've started, just in the last couple of years, giving money to an organization that works with abused kids. I think that's part of my recognition that it happened to me, because I don't think I've really been able to recognize or acknowledge it. I'm not comfortable saying I was abused. I feel that it taints me. I don't want people to conclude that I'm therefore such-and-so because I had that experience.

If I met a kid who was in a violent family, I'd say, "Look, kid, it's really tough. It's not something you're bringing on yourself, and it will end. And be careful not to pass it on just because you've been handed it."

BULLETIN BOARD

Child Abuse

Number of cases of child abuse and neglect reported in the United States in 1992: 2.9 million

Number of reported cases of physical abuse: 783,000

Number of reported cases of sexual abuse: 493,000

Number of reported cases of child neglect: 1,305,000

Number of reported cases of emotional abuse: 203,000

Number of reported cases of abandonment or other forms of abuse: 116,000

Number of children abused and neglected in 1992: 45 in 1,000

Number of children who died from abuse or neglect in 1992: over 1,200

Number of children who die from abuse each day: 2 to 5

Source: National Center on Child Abuse Prevention, a program of The National Center for Prevention of Child Abuse, 1992 survey.

Estimated number of cases of child abuse and neglect not reported each year: 3 million

Frequency of attacks on children: every 13 seconds

Number of children seriously abused each year: about 1.5 million

Percentage of abused children who are under six years old: 40%

Percentage of abuse cases that involve the parent's use of alcohol or drugs: 40%

Spouse Abuse

Number of women beaten to death by their partners each year: 2,000 to 4,000

Number of marriages in which some form of violence occurs: 1 in 4

Percentage of abusive husbands who also abuse their children: 70%

Abuse of the Elderly

Number of elderly persons abused or neglected each year: 1 in 25

Percentage of victims who are abused by their adult children: 30%

Sexual Abuse

Number of children sexually abused each year: 2 in 1,000

Average age of a sexually abused child: 10 years old

Number of Americans who have been sexually abused: 1 in 6

Estimated percentage of families in which there's been incest: 14%

Sources: Berger, Gilda. *Violence and the Family.* Watts, 1990.

Lee H. Bowker, Michelle Arbitell, and J. Richard McFerron. "On the Relationship Between Wife Beating and Child Abuse." In *Feminist Perspectives on Wife Abuse,* Kersti Yllö and Michele Bogard, eds. Sage, 1988.

Hyde, Margaret. *Know About Abuse.* Walker, 1992.

Park, Angela. *Child Abuse.* Watts, 1988.

Violence Update (1993), quoted by ChildHelp USA, 1994.

Communicating

Q My dad treats my brother and me badly. I think he's abusing us. What do I do about it? Can I tell total strangers what goes on inside my house? Are they going to believe me? I thought that what goes on in a house is supposed to be private.

A What goes on in a house is private, but only up to a certain point. Do you think it would be a private matter if your father decided not to feed you anymore, or if he refused to let you go to school?

Q No, that would be against the law. He'd get in trouble for that.

A The same is true if he abuses you.

Q But he says the reason he hits me is to teach me a lesson. He says it's my fault that I get hit. Parents have the right to punish their kids when they do something wrong, don't they?

A Parents have the right and the duty to discipline their children but not to abuse them. Beating is never appropriate punishment—for anything. Every year, thousands of young people are killed or permanently disabled at the hands of their parents. If your father isn't stopped, things could get much worse. When was the last time you got hit?

Q Yesterday. I came home a half-hour late from school. My dad was really angry, and he beat me pretty bad. I got a black eye.

A Do you know what his day was like yesterday?

Q Well, he's been out of work for nearly a year. He hasn't had much luck finding a new job. I know he's been drinking a lot. He and Mom have had some major fights over how much time he's spending at the bar. I guess he was pretty drunk yesterday.

A Do you think that his hitting you might have had something to do with something besides you? Is it possible that he was just frustrated and angry and drunk, and you happened to come in at a bad time?

Q Yeah, maybe . . . but I was late.

A And, for being a half-hour late from school, do you think you deserved a beating and a black eye? Does that sound like a fair punishment?

Q I guess not.

A It sounds as if it's your father who has the problem, not you. It sounds as if you'd be doing the whole family a favor if you were to get some help. Do you think you can talk to a social worker at a child protective service in your area?

Q I'd be afraid to.

A Well, then, maybe you want to start with an adult friend—your mother or a close relative, perhaps, or maybe a teacher or school counselor. You could even talk to a friend's mother or father.

Q What do I say?

A Explain what's going on. Explain that you think you and your family need help.

Q What if the person doesn't believe me?

A There's a chance that'll happen. If it does, tell someone else. What's happening is real. Some people just refuse to believe it. If you can't find an adult friend to help you out, you'll have to go to the authorities by yourself. Don't worry that they won't believe you. Child welfare workers and police officers hear stories like yours every day. They know you're not making this up.

Q What happens if I don't tell?

A Chances are, your father will become more abusive to you, your brother, and your mother. If he's already drinking too much, you can see that he's abusing himself; his self-abuse may become worse, too.

Maybe you think things can't get better, but they can. It may take a bit of time and may get harder before it gets easier, but in the end, it will be over. If you do nothing, it may never be over.

• • • • • • • • • • •

Making Your Decision

You need to decide whether or not you're going to tell someone what's going on. A good way to start making your decision is to gather all the facts you can. Maybe if you knew more about violence within families and child abuse, you'd understand how serious it is. Go to the library and read some books or magazines about abuse. Call a few hot lines—some are listed at the back of this book—and talk to some counselors there. You won't have to give your name. If you want, they may be able to send you some written information

Discussing the abuse in your home may at first be very difficult. You may want to start out talking with someone you know fairly well and can trust, like a schoolteacher.

about child abuse. If you're afraid your father might find the brochures if they are sent to your house, have them sent to a friend's house. A local hot line might even be able to direct you to a peer support group for young people who are going through what you're going through.

Find out what the authorities do when someone reports a case of child abuse. Find out what happens to the abuser and to the family. Then decide whether it makes sense to report what's going on in your family.

Thinking It Through

■ First, examine the facts. If you don't say anything, what will your home life be like for you, your brothers or sisters, your mother, and your father? What does your research say about your future—about emotional and other problems you may have when you grow up? What else could you do to make things better for yourself? If you do report the abuse, does it look as if you and your family can get help? What is likely to happen to your father? You might even want to write a list of the pros and cons of reporting your father's behavior.

■ Second, examine your feelings. How does it feel when you go home? How do you feel about your father? Do you think that telling might help him or hurt him? What do you think your mother is going through? Are you scared to tell? Which do you think is harder: being beaten by your father or going through all that you'll have to go through?

■ Finally, make your decision.

Communicating Your Decision

Making the decision to tell is hard, but actually telling will be hard, too. Let's say you decide to talk to a child protective services worker about what's going on. If you plan ahead for the conversation, you can make it a little easier.

Planning the Conversation

It's natural to feel that what goes on in your family is a private matter. And it's natural to think that you're somehow "ratting" on your father by telling, but you know that he's out of control. By talking to the authorities, you'll be helping him. Keep reminding yourself of that to give yourself the courage to speak up.

Some people find it hard to say certain things aloud, no matter how many times they've rehearsed them in their heads. If that's true for you, you might want to practice your conversation with a friend. Role-play; pretend the friend is the social worker with whom you're planning to talk, and tell your story.

Having the Conversation

It can help to start the conversation by telling the social worker what you're most worried about. If you're afraid of what will happen when your father finds out what you've done, ask about that. If you're worried about what will happen to your father in the end, ask about that. You might want the social worker to describe exactly what happens after you make the report. That way, you'll know what to expect.

Then tell your story. Don't exaggerate anything or hide anything. Be absolutely honest about what's happening. You may surprise yourself as you tell your story. Many young people who report their abuse go into the conversation thinking that things aren't really so bad at home and that it was a mistake to come. But as they talk, they realize how much they've suffered. Only when they tell a stranger what their life is like do they fully realize how much abuse they've been through.

After you've spoken, give the social worker a chance to respond. And *listen* to what he or she says. Chances are, the social worker will tell you that it's not your fault, that it was a wise move to tell, and that, because you've told, things will get better. Stop and listen to those words. Accept them as true

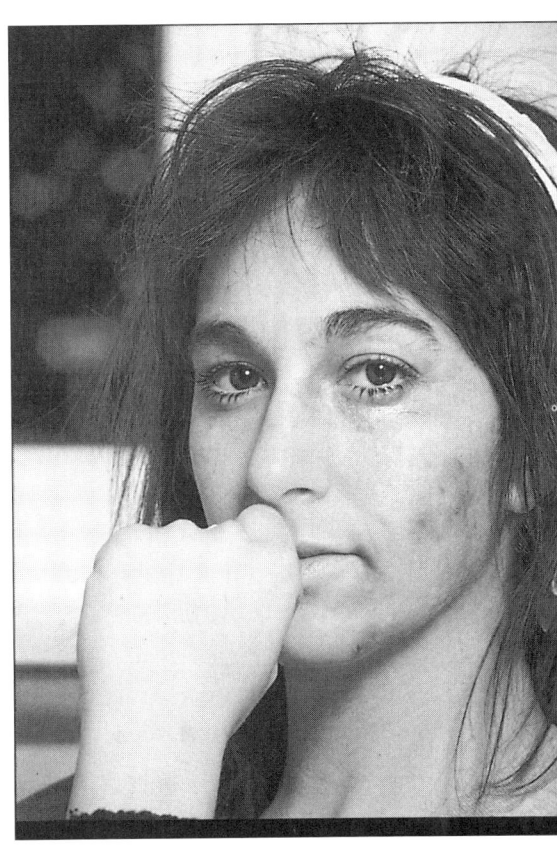

Evidence of physical abuse is shocking and unmistakable. If a man is hitting his wife, his whole family may be in danger of abuse.

for just a few minutes, and see if they make sense. If they do, then believe them.

Sticking to Your Decision
Once you've made your decision and reported the abuse, there will be an investigation and a follow-up. When he finds out what you've done, your father may be upset. He may threaten you or demand that you take back what you've said.

■ Don't let him talk you into taking anything back. Don't let him convince you that nothing is happening or that what is happening isn't bad. If he or anyone threatens you, tell the social worker about it, and ask for protection.

■ Commit yourself. Remind yourself that you're reporting this to make your home better for everyone in your family, including your father. If you're going to do it, don't do it halfway. Don't cover anything up or take back what you've said. Cooperate fully with the authorities. Go into counseling if that's recommended for you.

■ Don't put yourself in further danger. Find out from the authorities what to do if your father attacks you again. Ask for addresses of places where you can go if you do get hit. You might want to ask friends if you can stay at their houses if you need to. Report any further attacks to the authorities.

No matter how you decide to handle it, making the decision on your own and taking care of yourself are the first steps toward taking control of your life. When you make a decision and stick to it, you'll feel good about yourself.

Families and Violence

Q My name is Francesca. My mom is always threatening me. She waves knives around and throws dishes at me. She says terrible things to me, like, "I'm going to kill you," and "I wish you were never born." I know parents get angry, and I know I'm not always good, but it's gotten so bad that I'm afraid to go home. What should I do?

A Many people, when they think of child abuse, think of physical abuse, such as beating and slapping. But many children are seriously abused without ever getting hit. Not all abuse is physical. Your mom is threatening you and saying very hurtful things. She is making your home a scary place. If what she says and does makes you afraid to go home, your mom may be abusing you emotionally. You should find an adult to talk to about this right away.

• • • • • • • • • • • •

As you can probably tell, verbal and emotional abuse can be just as painful as physical abuse—sometimes it's even more painful. Your home is supposed to be your safe place, a place you can go when you're tired, scared, upset, or need comfort. And your mom is supposed to be your protector, the one to go to when someone or something else scares you.

Your mom needs help, and so do you. Chances are that she means well and doesn't want to hurt you. She just has trouble being a mom sometimes. Many kids are afraid to say anything about what's going on because they want to protect their parents, and they're scared about what would happen to the family if they told. You may be afraid you'll get your mom in some sort of trouble. Don't be. Once you report the problem, you'll get help from people who will work to keep your mom together with you and your family in a healthier and safer way.

Emotional Abuse from Parents

It often takes longer to heal an emotional wound than a cut or a broken bone. Emotional abuse also is often harder for a person to tell anyone about. That's why many people don't report it. They think that no one is going to believe that they are being abused unless they can show broken bones, bruises, or other physical evidence of what's happening to them. Some people think that, so long as they're not being physically hurt, they're not really being harmed. But they are wrong. You would be wrong, too, not to do something to change what's going on with your mom.

Emotional abuse can cause long-term damage. Also, if you don't say anything, it may get worse. Many emotionally abusive parents get more and more abusive; many will eventually take their frustrations out through physical violence. If you say and do nothing, things may get worse at home.

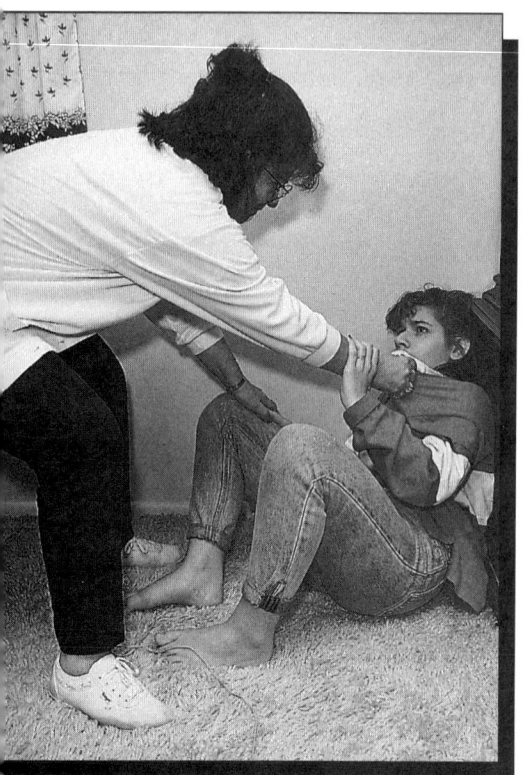

An adult who abuses a child may cause serious emotional damage as well as physical damage.

Verbal Abuse

Some emotional abuse is verbal. It is most commonly directed against older children and teenagers, although it can happen to children of any age. Some parents badger their children, repeatedly calling them ugly or stupid or saying, "I hate you." Some parents constantly threaten their children with harm or blame them for family problems.

Children—even teenagers—are emotionally dependent on their parents. They pay attention to and can react strongly to what their parents say and do. If your parents are saying abusive things to you, even if you think you're "tuning out" those remarks, you are hearing them, and they are having an effect. A single, isolated comment from a parent usually has little effect on a child. But if you hear such hurtful comments every day or over a long period of time, you will begin to believe them—and that can be devastating to your emotional growth.

Beyond Verbal Abuse

Some emotional abuse is more than just verbal. Some parents abuse their children through public humiliation. Mitch was eight years old, and he was still having a lot of trouble with bed-wetting. His parents decided to punish him by making him announce his problem to their family and all their friends. Every time a friend came over, Mitch's mom would ask, "And what did you do last night, Mitch?" Not only did this not cure his bed-wetting problem, but it also had a lasting effect on Mitch. He became more withdrawn and less eager to spend time with his friends.

Another, very serious, form of emotional abuse is seeing someone else in the family be abused. Children who see a parent, brother, sister, or other family member constantly hit or yelled at often suffer just as much as the one being attacked. They may feel bad to see someone else suffer, guilty that they cannot stop the suffering, and afraid that they will be next to suffer the same abuse.

Neglect

Parents have certain responsibilities toward their children. They must provide them with the proper food and clothing. They must make sure their children receive proper medical care, education, and supervision. If they don't, they are guilty of child neglect. This is true whether the parents acted on purpose or by accident.

What counts as neglect of a child depends on the circumstances. "Proper food and clothing," for example, doesn't mean the very best food and clothing there is. It means "appropriate food and clothing," considering the family's financial abilities and other circumstances. It doesn't mean a mother must pay $100 for athletic shoes for her daughter, but it does mean that her daughter must have shoes of some sort. And, if they live in a winter climate, the daughter would need boots as well.

Is it neglect to leave a child at home alone? That depends on the age and maturity of the child as well as the length of time he or she is left alone. It would be neglect to leave a two-year-old alone for even a short time. It might be acceptable to leave a 12-year-old alone for an afternoon, but certainly not for an entire week.

In addition to these physical and educational needs, a child has emotional needs. A child who does not receive love, affection, and sufficient attention may be a victim of emotional neglect. A parent who never says a kind word, never gives a hug or a kiss, or gives his or her child "the silent treatment" can make that child feel worthless, with emotional scars that can last into adulthood.

Abuse and Discipline

Parents have a duty to set limits for their children and correct them when they misbehave. Sometimes parents have to discipline their children. And different parents use different methods of discipline. Some take away television or telephone privileges. Others assign extra chores. Still others yell at their children or slap or spank them.

While discipline is an important part of parenting, sometimes it gets out of control. Punishment should teach, but it should not hurt. While a small amount of physical punishment is acceptable by many in today's society, it's not always a good idea. Sometimes parents mean well and simply want to teach their child a lesson but lose control. They may end up hurting the child badly.

There's a rule in the American legal system that the punishment must fit the crime. This is true in families, too. If you were being careless and dropped and broke a dinner plate, it might be appropriate for your parents to make you wash the dishes for a week or pay for the plate out of your own money. It would be inappropriate to receive a severe beating or to be sent to your room without dinner for a week.

Accidents

Parents are only human, and accidents do happen. A parent may accidentally bump a child or turn away for a minute in the kitchen, giving a curious child an opportunity to touch a hot stove. Innocent mishaps like these are not abuse.

Abuse, whether deliberate or caused by negligence, is most often a pattern of behavior. While a single, deliberate, harmful act might be considered abuse, the great majority of abuse takes place over an extended period of time.

Other Abusive Family Relationships

Abuse within the family isn't limited to a parent hurting a child. Abuse happens to people of all ages, and it can happen whenever anyone is in a position of power over another person. Children may be abused by their parents, by their parents' spouses, boyfriends or girlfriends, or friends, or by others in the family. Outside the home, children may be abused by teachers, day-care workers, neighbors, or other adults or older children. Adults may also be abused by family members or other people they spend time with.

Sibling Abuse

Billy's parents made him babysit his little brother Mick every Friday. Billy hated it; he was 15 years old and wanted to spend Friday nights with his friends. Pleading with his parents and trying to come up with compromises didn't work, so Billy took his anger out on Mick. As soon as their parents left, Billy would attack Mick, kicking and punching him. Once, when it was especially important for him to see some friends, he tied Mick up in his bedroom and left the house.

We all have fights with our brothers and sisters from time to time. Jealousy, rivalries, and fights among siblings are common. These disagreements usually don't last long and can be worked out without anyone getting hurt.

Sometimes, however, an older brother or sister can become abusive. This is especially common if that older sibling has also been a victim of abuse. It can also happen when the older sibling has some form of power over or responsibility for the younger one, as in the case of Billy and Mick.

Spouse Abuse

Millions of women are beaten and abused each year by the men they live with. (There are men who are abused by women, but these cases are more rare.) Such abuse is not only devastating to the woman, it's also extremely harmful to the children who live with her and to others who love her.

In some households, a man may force the children to watch as he abuses their mother. He may do this to remind the children who's "in charge."

Even if they don't witness the attack, children might see their mother after the attack when she is crying or bruised. Watching or hearing a parent be abused can be as upsetting as being abused yourself. Many children in this situation feel guilty, thinking it's something they did that caused their mom to get hit.

Why do women stay with men who abuse them or their children? Many stay because they think leaving might be even worse. They may fear that the man will injure or kill them. They may be dependent on the man for financial support. Especially when they are raising small children, they don't see any way they could survive on their own.

Many women have found safety from spousal abuse for themselves and their children in local shelters for battered women. There they receive support, counseling, and legal advice.

Often, they don't have the confidence to go out on their own. Many abused women are so used to being berated that they believe it when the partner says, "You'd never make it without me." Some don't leave because of religious or cultural reasons. Others feel the abuse is their fault or that they deserve the treatment they get. Not only will these women not tell anyone about their circumstances, they will lie when they are asked if anything is wrong. Quite often, these women don't know about the resources available to them, such as shelters and support centers. When women do seek aid at such resource centers—and fortunately many do—they learn ways to break out of their abusive situations.

Abuse of the Elderly
Abigail is 77 years old. She lives alone in an apartment three miles from her daughter, Sheryl. Sheryl is unmarried, with a full-time job and three small children. As Abigail has gotten older and weaker, she has come to depend more and more upon Sheryl.

In addition to all her duties at home and at work, Sheryl now does all of her mother's shopping, cooking, and laundry. Sheryl has begun to resent doing all this extra work. Sometimes when she's very angry, she "accidentally on purpose" forgets to go over and make dinner. Sometimes she gives her mother extra sleeping pills so her mother will sleep through the day and not bother her. Once or twice, when her temper was really short, Sheryl hit her mother to keep her quiet.

When people grow older, they may require a lot of care from others. Whether they live alone, with their children, or in a care center for the elderly, many elderly people face abuse from those who are supposed to love them and care for them. They may be abused by their spouses, by their children, by people who live with them, or by people who are employed to care for them. The abusers may neglect them or overmedicate them, as Sheryl did. They may also physically abuse them or steal from them.

Why do these elderly people put up with it? Like young children, very frail elderly people are dependent on their caregivers. Some become confused, forgetful, and depressed and don't understand what is going on. Even if they do understand, they may feel that saying something may make things worse rather than better.

The Cycle of Abuse
Unfortunately, a person who is abused often turns around and abuses others. For example, women beaten by their husbands may slap their children or take their frustrations out on elderly family members. Children who are abused often abuse younger siblings, pets, or other children. Boys who grow up

around abusive fathers may abuse their girlfriends, and these girls, if they grew up around abuse, may simply learn to live with it. This cycle of abuse, if not stopped, may continue generation after generation. Family therapists can show family members how to change this destructive behavior and break the cycle of abuse.

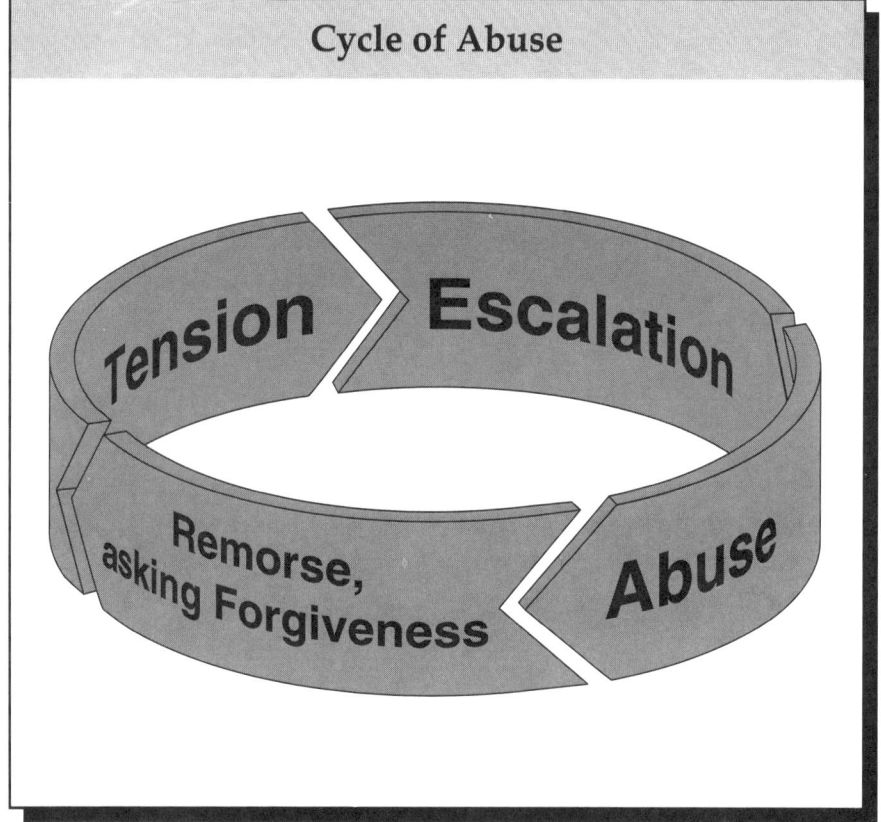

Abuse typically occurs in a cycle. This cycle makes it very confusing for the the victim of abuse. He or she is often hurt and then asked for forgiveness over and over again.

The Causes of Violence

Q My name's Carlos. My dad failed to get a promotion at work six months ago, and ever since, he's been scary to be around. He yells at my mom and hits my brother and me. I know it's hard for him to deal with, but why does he take it out on us?

A You're right; your father is going through a hard time. He feels disappointed and put down, and he's taking it out on you. He probably deserved the promotion and was counting on the extra money. He has a lot of responsibilities and worries, such as how he's going to earn enough money in these times to support his family.

• • • • • • • • • • • •

None of this is an excuse for violence, however. What he is doing to you, your mother, and your brother is not okay. Your father is dealing with his frustrations and problems in the wrong way. He has to learn to deal with his emotions in a healthy and safe way.

Your father needs help. Counselors and support groups can give him emotional help and advice. They can help him deal with his feelings or suggest the possibility of a job change. Once he reaches out, he'll find many people who are willing to help him.

You and your family need help, too. The abuse has to stop right away. Talk to your mother or another adult about what's going on. The sooner you do, the sooner it can stop.

It's very important that you understand that what your father is doing is not your fault. Don't feel guilty for what he's doing, and don't make excuses for his behavior. At times, your father may try to blame his behavior on you or something you did, but you have not brought this on.

Even if your father later apologizes to you, don't let it end there. Tell him that what he is doing is hurting you, and you need it to stop.

Who Abuses?

Violence happens in all types of families. It happens in wealthy families and poor families of all social, racial, and religious groups, in cities and rural areas. It happens in small and large

People who have lost their jobs and have trouble finding work often are angry and frustrated. They may need as much help in controlling their emotions at home as they do in finding new jobs.

families, in families with one parent or two, and in families living with grandparents, cousins, and other relatives.

Family violence is not always a case of a parent abusing a child. Children are abused by grandparents, brothers, sisters, other relatives, babysitters, and friends and boyfriends/girlfriends of parents. Children are also abused by adoptive parents and stepparents as well as biological parents. And adults are often abused by their spouses or by their grown children.

There is no one profile of abusers or abusive families. For this reason, never doubt a friend who says that he or she is being abused. When you know the person your friend is talking about, it may be hard to believe that "such a nice man" or "a professional woman like that" could be hurting someone—especially someone he or she loves. For the same reason, don't doubt your own feelings if you think you're being abused. People may try to tell you that it couldn't be happening, because it doesn't happen in families like yours. Unfortunately, it does.

The Causes of Violence

People rarely abuse other people just because they want to be cruel and harmful. Like Carlos's father, there is usually something causing the abuser to act that way. Most of the time, that "something" has nothing to do with the person who is being abused. The victim just happens to be in the wrong place at the wrong time.

Frustration and Stress

Parents face a lot of stressful times. For Carlos's father, failing to advance in his job was a burden that he was unable to handle in a healthy way. He took his anger out on his family.

Many people become overwhelmed by on-the-job stress. Others face personal difficulties, such as marital problems or too many demands on their time. Single parents, who have to juggle a job and family responsibilities without a partner, have extra stress to handle. Instead of finding a healthy outlet for their frustration, these people may lash out at others.

When times are difficult, some people feel the need to take their frustrations out on someone or something. When parents are under a lot of stress, a simple mistake from a child may be all it takes for them to blow up. The same pressures may cause husbands to abuse their wives or grown children to abuse their elderly parents.

Low Self-Esteem

People with low self-esteem don't have much respect for themselves. They feel powerless and unable to do anything. Some people suffer from low self-esteem all the time. Others feel this way when circumstances are going poorly for them, such as when they are unemployed or newly divorced.

Sometimes a person with low self-esteem looks for ways to feel powerful. Again, unfortunately, children and wives are an available target. Hitting someone smaller or weaker gives the person with low self-esteem a brief feeling of power. It makes the person feel that he or she has control over someone. In an effort to re-experience the feeling of power, the abuser may fall into a continual pattern of abusing the victim.

Substance Abuse

The use and abuse of alcohol and drugs make it difficult for people to control their behavior. Drugs and alcohol lessen people's self-control and reduce their ability to think or act rationally. About one in three cases of child abuse occurs when the abuser has been drinking. A great many more occur as a result of the use of crack (cocaine) and other addictive and dangerous substances.

As with many other aspects of family violence, substance abuse often leads to more substance abuse. For example, a woman who frequently suffers abuse from her husband may

During times of stress, some people turn to alcohol or drugs to make themselves feel better. They may also become depressed, angry, or irrational, however, and begin abusing their families.

begin drinking heavily. Her continuing dependence on alcohol increases the chance that she will in turn abuse her children.

Immaturity or Lack of Parenting Skills
May Wah was 15 when she had her baby. Her parents had thrown her out of the house when she got pregnant. She moved in with an older friend who had an apartment and worked as a waitress until the baby arrived. She knew nothing about taking care of a child. When the baby was nine months old, May Wah rushed him to the hospital. He was unconscious. The doctors asked May Wah what had happened. She told them, "When the baby cried, I thought the best thing was to teach him a lesson. I told him I wouldn't feed him until he quieted down." Since his hunger only made him cry more, she finally tried "shaking some sense into him." She shook him so hard that she caused permanent brain damage.

Many young parents have little experience with child care. This can lead to both physical and emotional abuse. Some inexperienced parents expect too much of their babies. They think babies should be able to reason and understand the way older children can. They become abusive when the babies "misbehave." Often, these new parents have little family support and may not know where to turn for help.

Isolation of the Family
Raising children is a time-consuming and long-term responsibility. Every parent needs a break now and then. For the parent who has had a hard day, just being able to ask a relative or friend to watch the child for a few hours can make a big difference. It can give the parent some time to unwind and relieve some stress.

Parents need not only practical support such as babysitting, but also emotional support. A single parent of toddlers needs to have other adults to talk to. A parent with a difficult teenager may benefit greatly from talking with someone else who has raised teenagers.

Unfortunately, many families are lacking that much needed support. Families in the United States today tend to be mobile. It's not uncommon for a family to travel to a neighboring state or even across the country for a new job. Many Americans are immigrants who live far away from their families and friends. Without that support system, these families often feel lonely and very isolated.

Some families are isolated even within their own communities. Abusive adults usually want to hide the injuries they cause to their spouses or children. They often closely monitor their wives' and children's activities and don't let them have many friendships.

Having contact with other people is an important part of a person's development. Denying a person this kind of contact is itself a form of emotional abuse. In addition, children and

Predictors of Domestic Violence

**Behaviors in Men That Indicate
Increased Likelihood of Wife Assault**

- ☐ Grew up in a violent family.

- ☐ Tends to use force or violence to "solve" problems. Punches walls or throws things. Is cruel to animals.

- ☐ Abuses alcohol or other drugs.

- ☐ Thinks poorly of himself. Tries to act tough.

- ☐ Has strong traditional ideas about what a man should be and what a woman should be.

- ☐ Is jealous of his wife, her family, and her male and female friends.

- ☐ Plays with knives or guns and threatens to use them to "get even."

- ☐ Expects his wife to follow orders and gets angry if she has not anticipated his wishes.

- ☐ Goes through extreme highs and lows of behaviors. (Extremely kind, extremely cruel.)

- ☐ Treats his wife roughly.

- ☐ Threatens his wife. As a result, his wife fears him when he is angry and spends most of her time trying not to make him angry.

Source: The National Coalition Against Domestic Violence.

adults who have limited contact with people outside the family may not realize that they're being mistreated. Even if they do realize it, they have few opportunities to tell someone outside what's going on in the home.

Social isolation is also dangerous for the abuser. Without help from counselors and support groups, abusers find it nearly impossible to overcome their problems. The longer they isolate themselves, the more completely they destroy themselves and their families.

Causes of Neglect

While abuse is most often a physical or emotional action, neglect is usually *inaction*—not doing what you're expected to do. Many of the same factors that cause abusive behavior may lead to neglect.

For example, inexperienced parents like May Wah may not know what to do with a child. When the child becomes sick, they may neglect to take the child to a doctor. The same is true for parents who were neglected by their own parents—they may not know how a caring parent is supposed to behave.

Some parents—especially those who are immature, abuse drugs or alcohol, or are distracted by other personal problems—have trouble taking care of themselves. They may survive on potato chips and coffee or may spend a week in bed. These parents frequently are also guilty of neglecting their children. Their children may not get fed or may get "whatever's around." An infant, for example, might be given a bottle of soda instead of a bottle of formula. In very severe cases, parents like these might even abandon a child.

Some neglectful parents may not even realize they're being neglectful. Some inexperienced parents treat their children as miniature adults. They expect the children to be capable of caring for themselves and, often, their siblings. They may leave a six-year-old in charge of a three-year-old, for example, and think that the older child will be able to feed and care for the younger one.

Another major cause of child neglect is mental illness, such as severe depression or schizophrenia. Mental illness makes it hard, sometimes impossible, for a person to cope with everyday responsibilities and realities. Mentally ill parents may go through periods when they lose track of time, are disoriented, or are otherwise unable to look after themselves or take care of their children.

A Special Case: Children with Disabilities

Another common victim of abuse, sadly enough, is the child with physical or mental disabilities. A child with a disability is more likely to suffer abuse than other children.

There are a number of reasons why this is true. First, children with physical or mental disabilities require more attention than other children. This may compound the problems that the parents have, making them even more frustrated and unable to cope.

Second, children with disabilities—especially those with mental disabilities—develop differently from other children. Unfortunately, parents don't always understand how far their children can develop. They may demand the same behavior from a disabled child that they do from other children. As the child grows physically and does not grow in the same way mentally, the parent's pushing may become abusive. This is why parents with disabled children need to be given special training and knowledge about their children.

CHAPTER 4

Sexual Abuse—A Form of Violence

Q I'm Melissa. I think my uncle touches me in a way that's wrong, but I'm not sure. He says we're just cuddling, but it bothers me. I'm scared that he may be doing the same thing to my little sister. Is what he does okay? Should I say anything?

A No, what he does is not okay, and yes, you should say something—the sooner the better. You should say something right away, and you should continue saying it until your uncle stops touching you.

• • • • • • • • • • •

Everyone enjoys physical contact with friends and family members. A hug or kiss from someone you love can make you feel warm and happy. These kinds of touching are OK, but some kinds are not. If you feel that "something is funny" in the way that your uncle touches you, you are probably right. Even if you don't believe that your uncle would ever harm you, trust your feelings. Deep inside, you know what kinds of touching are not OK.

Whenever someone tries to touch you in a way that makes you uncomfortable, you have the right to say no. You have the right to say, "That part of my body is private. Don't touch me there." The other person must listen to you.

If your uncle doesn't stop when you tell him to, look for help from someone else. Your uncle's behavior is not your fault. Telling another person may be hard to do. But you do have to talk about it—if not for your own good, then for the good of your sister. Your uncle may be doing the same thing to her. Even if he isn't doing it now, he may do it in the future.

Forms of Sexual Abuse

The behavior of Melissa's uncle is sexual abuse. Sexual abuse means taking advantage of someone in a sexual way. People of all ages, from infancy to adulthood, and of both sexes may be victims of sexual abuse.

Physical Abuse
Most sexual abuse is physical. The abuser may touch or rub the victim's genitals, breasts, or other sexual areas. The victim may be told to touch the abuser in sexual places. Touching may be done with the fingers, the mouth, or other parts of the body.

Any sexual activity between an adult and a minor (a person below the legal age of adulthood) is considered sexual abuse. If that activity takes place between members of the same family, it is called incest.

Quite often, abusers who get away with one form of sexual abuse become bolder. They may start with hugging or "cuddling," then begin fondling and sexual touching. If they are not stopped, they may move into sexual intercourse.

Nonphysical Abuse
Not all sexual abuse involves touching. Adults may ask a young person to watch them perform sexual acts or look at sexual pictures. Some adults like to look at a child's nude body or take pictures of children in sexual poses. Some adults get sexual pleasure from exhibitionism—walking around naked or "flashing" their genitals at someone. Nonphysical abuse can be just as damaging emotionally as physical abuse.

A child who is sexually abused may feel so threatened or worried that she cannot refuse her abuser. She is also afraid that nobody will believe her if she tells on him.

Marital Rape

Although children and teenagers are the most common victims of sexual abuse within families, they are not the only victims. Some wives are victims of a common kind of sexual abuse called marital rape.

Rape means forcing a person to have sexual intercourse. Some married men believe they have the right to have sex with their wives whenever they want. Legally, however, they do not have this right. A husband who forces his wife to have sex against her will is committing an act of rape.

Why It Happens

Adults abuse young people sexually for many reasons. Some have emotional problems that make them want to mistreat young people. Others lose control over themselves because of alcohol or drug problems.

Most sexual abuse against minors is committed by someone the minor knows or trusts. In families, the most common abusers are fathers, stepfathers, or other male relatives who visit frequently. (Women don't often commit sexual abuse.) Older siblings, other children or teenagers, family friends, and babysitters may also be sexually abusive.

In some cases, sexual abuse happens only once. Often, however, an adult will continue to abuse a minor sexually over a long period of time.

How Can They Do It?

Most adults understand that sexual contact with young people is harmful and wrong. Most parents promote healthy family behavior that makes the expression of affection among family members not a matter of fear or worry but comfort and support. Common sense governs, and sexual feelings are naturally controlled.

In some families, however, such common sense has not been

practiced among family members. Sexual abuse can be the result, and some adults just don't care about the damage they are causing.

For example, a man with a frustrating or unrewarding job may feel the need to have power over someone. He may rape his wife or sexually abuse his daughter. A man whose wife is absent, ill, or unwilling to have sex may ask his daughter to fulfill his desires. Unlike the wife, the daughter may be too confused or afraid to say no.

Some adults really do care about the harm their sexual abuse might cause. To make themselves feel better, they "rationalize," or make up excuses for their behavior instead of stopping it. They try to convince their victims—and themselves—that their actions aren't really sexual abuse.

For example, some fathers tell their daughters that their sexual advances are a way to show how much they love them. Others say that it's a father's duty to teach his daughter about sex. Others say that sexual activity with their daughters is harmless, so long as it doesn't go all the way to intercourse. Still others say that it's a father's natural right to have sex with his daughter. All of these excuses are false—and deep inside, both the abuser and the victim know it.

You Are Not Responsible

Anything having to do with sex can be confusing and scary to young people. Very young children know nothing about sex. Older children learn what it's about, but they're usually told that it's something secret or bad. Eventually, they begin experimenting with sex and are curious to learn more. The message is unclear: is sex something good or something bad?

Some adults take advantage of this confusion. They claim that children ask for sex. Abusers sometimes say that a boy or girl made sexual advances that they couldn't resist. The child in these cases isn't necessarily a teenager. Some child abusers

Child Abuse in the United States

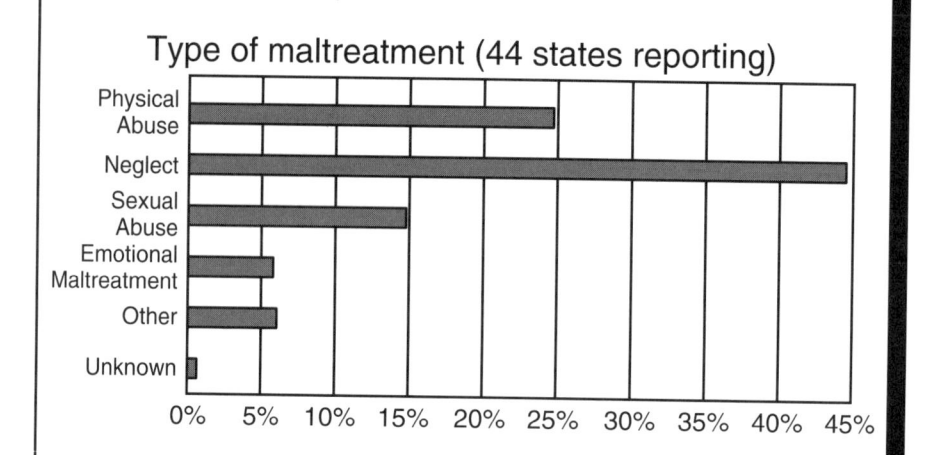

Type of maltreatment (44 states reporting)

Category	Percent
Physical Abuse	~25%
Neglect	~45%
Sexual Abuse	~15%
Emotional Maltreatment	~5%
Other	~6%
Unknown	<1%

Percent of child victims by age (46 states reporting)

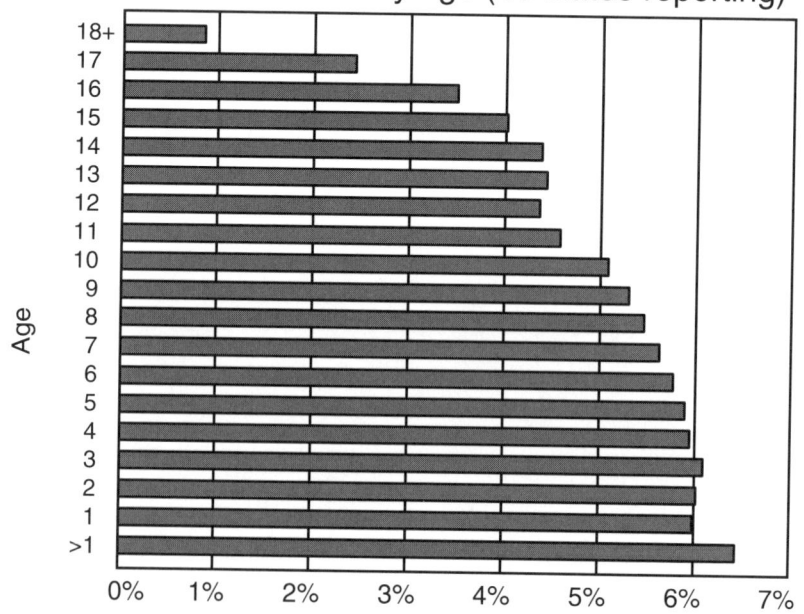

Age	Percent
18+	~1%
17	~2.5%
16	~3.5%
15	~4%
14	~4.5%
13	~4.5%
12	~4.5%
11	~5%
10	~5%
9	~5.5%
8	~5.5%
7	~5.5%
6	~5.5%
5	~6%
4	~6%
3	~6%
2	~6%
1	~6%
>1	~6.5%

Source: National Child Abuse and Neglect Data System, Working Paper 1, 1990 Summary Data Component, National Center on Child Abuse and Neglect, (Washington, DC, 1992).

actually talk about six-year-olds or five-year-olds who were asking for sex.

These abusers want to hold the victims responsible for their abuse. But a minor can never be held responsible for sexual activity with an adult. Even in cases when a child or teenager "comes on" sexually to an adult, the adult has the responsibility to say no. Any adult who has sexual relations with a minor, for any reason, is committing a crime.

Force and Consent

When adults abuse young people sexually, they very rarely have to use physical violence. Most children and teenagers agree to do what the abuser asks; they are not beaten or pushed. There are many forms of pressure that are as strong as, or stronger than, physical force.

Threats and Intimidation

Instead of actually using force, some abusers simply threaten to hurt their victims. They may also threaten to hurt others in the family if the victim does not agree to sexual contact.

Usually, however, the abuser's threats are much less violent. For example, Bruce started abusing his daughter Ilona when she was six years old. By the time Ilona was eight, she realized she didn't like his nighttime visits. She told him to stop. Bruce said that if Ilona didn't let him touch her this way, he'd leave the family. He said they'd starve to death without him, and it would be her fault. Thinking she had no other choice, Ilona let him continue the abuse.

Even if the abuser doesn't make threats, young people may imagine terrible consequences if they don't cooperate. Some teenagers, like Melissa, may agree to an abuser's requests because they're worried he'll abuse a younger brother or sister.

Most often, children who are approached by a parent for a sexual encounter see the parent's request as a demand. They don't realize they have the power to refuse. Younger children are especially dependent on the adults who care for them. When a parent or other adult says to do something, the child usually just does it.

Bribes

Some young people are bribed into performing sexual acts or sexual favors. Josie's uncle gave his "favorite niece" special treats. He took her on trips without her brothers and sisters. Josie felt special and enjoyed the extra attention. Even though she hated her uncle's sexual fondling, she was willing to put up with it because of what she got in return. In time she may lose all motivation to put an end to it.

Mothers' Reactions

Some sexual abusers are widowed or divorced men. With no adult woman in the house, they can abuse their children sexually without fear of interference. More often, however, there is a mother living at home. Why doesn't she stop her husband from committing sexual abuse?

In some cases, the woman simply is not aware of what her husband is doing. He keeps the activity a secret and bullies the child into doing the same. Even if the woman suspects that something is going on, she may be afraid to investigate. She doesn't want to find out that the man she married is hurting their child. Instead of facing the truth, she ignores the clues and suspicious activities. She may even refuse to listen to what her child tells her.

Some wives know what's going on but do nothing to stop the abuse. A woman may be afraid of what her husband would do if she tried to interfere.

A woman who was abused in childhood may even rationalize her husband's behavior. As a girl, she may have been told that sex with her father was a family responsibility or a sign of love. She may still believe these things as an adult, even though she remembers how much she resented what her father did to her.

Talking About It

Sexual abuse is one of the hardest things to talk about. Most young people don't want to speak up out of fear, shame, embarrassment, guilt, or loyalty to a family member. If you are being abused sexually, you are being harmed. You are keeping an ugly and dangerous secret. The sooner you begin to tell people about it, the sooner the abuse can be stopped. By talking about it, you can also protect other young people from going through what you've gone through. Most sexual abusers, if they get away with abusing one victim, will abuse others.

Letting It Continue

Some young victims of sexual abuse may let years go by without saying a word. They let an "accidental" touch or two go by without saying anything. The next thing they know, those touches have developed into sexual relations. The victims then feel that it's too late to complain. They think that because they didn't say anything earlier, they must be partly to blame. Therefore, they continue to suffer in silence.

If you are being sexually abused, you should realize that it's never too late to bring it to someone's attention. Whether the abuse has gone on for three days or three years, you are not responsible for it. Talking about sexual abuse is a courageous thing to do; some people just take longer than others to work up the courage.

Whom to Tell

Whom should you talk to about sexual abuse? If it is difficult to approach an adult, start by talking it out with a classmate or friend. Practice will make it easier to bring up again. You must find a way to tell an adult what's going on. When Kevin told his mother that his father was touching him in a funny way, she took action. She confronted her husband. She made him leave the house and told him he could only move back in after he'd had counseling. Until then, he could visit with Kevin only when she was present.

Unfortunately, not all parents are as supportive as Kevin's mom. Often, a mother will be ashamed of what her husband has done and will feel partly responsible. She'll refuse to take action out of fear that people will think she's a bad parent or a bad wife.

Other parents may refuse to admit that there's a problem. They'll say that their children are making up stories, that they must have asked for the treatment they're getting, or that they're exaggerating what's going on. They refuse to confront the abuser, and so the abuse continues.

If you tell a parent and he or she does nothing, don't stop there. Keep finding people to talk to until someone takes you seriously. If you can't talk to people you know, talk to a counselor. Look in the phone book for the number of the local child protective services

Counselors know whom to call and how to start helping someone who is being sexually abused. They know that the child is not at fault and that the abuse must be stopped immediately.

office, teen hot line, or rape crisis center. There are people at all of these offices who can help you.

The Effects of Sexual Abuse

The negative effects of child sexual abuse begin right away and can continue throughout adult life. Children and teenagers may have difficulty trusting other people and often experience terrible shame. They often become depressed. Their depression makes it hard for them to study or to pay attention at school. Some victims of sexual abuse develop terrible headaches and have frequent nightmares. Sometimes these symptoms begin right away; sometimes they appear years after the abuse has stopped.

Some young people react to their abuse by becoming withdrawn and insecure. They develop a poor self-image and may no longer take pleasure in the activities they used to enjoy. Many abused children become suicidal or run away from home and end up on the streets.

Girls who were forced into sexual activity by their fathers or other older men may have problems when they become adults. They often find it difficult to have lasting relationships with men. Some are disgusted by men and want nothing to do with them. Others become promiscuous and want to have sex with every man they can. (Many prostitutes were sexually abused as children.)

Young people who were sexually abused are more likely than others to abuse drugs or alcohol or to develop eating disorders. They are also more likely to abuse their own children.

Counseling can help people overcome many of the problems brought on by sexual abuse. Prevention, however, is always best: the sooner you can stop the abuse, the sooner you will be able to get over it.

CHAPTER 5

Doing Something About It

Q: My name's Jim. My mom hits me all the time. She says it's my fault. She says I misbehave, and I deserve the treatment I get. Do I really deserve to get beaten?

A: No. No one ever deserves to get beaten. But when your mom says it's your fault, it's only natural for you to believe her. You have no reason to think she'd do anything to hurt you. So when she says she hit you because you've misbehaved, you figure you really must have misbehaved.

• • • • • • • • • • • •

But maybe you should look more closely at what your mom is doing. You say she hits you "all the time." Do you really misbehave all the time? If you suddenly became the perfect son, do you really think your mom would never hit you again?

It sounds as if your mother is making excuses for her violent behavior. It's possible that she's attacking you because of something that's upsetting her—something that has nothing to do with you. She may be taking her anger out on you because you're an easy target.

Understanding What's Happening

It's hard for young people who are abused or neglected to understand why their parents would hurt them. Like Jim, many battered children are told that the beatings are their fault. They've been taught since infancy that their parents would never do anything wrong. For this reason, they tend to believe their parents' excuses.

Naturally, these young people expect that the abuse will stop as soon as they behave properly. So they may try to be perfectly good. They'll tiptoe around the house, trying desperately not to cause any trouble. Even then, nothing changes. They find themselves beaten no matter how well they try to behave.

Why does this happen? Usually, it's because the abuse has nothing to do with the child's behavior. Like Jim's mother, the parents are venting their anger on the closest, most vulnerable target. It makes no difference whether or not that target was the real cause of the anger.

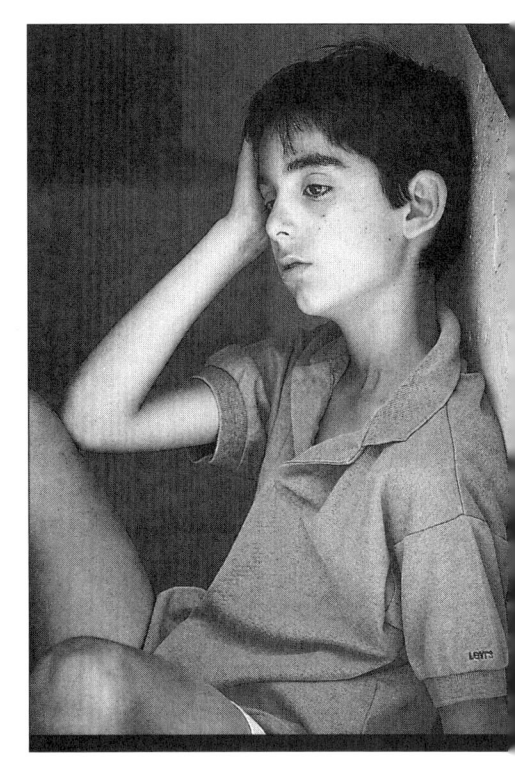

A child who constantly experiences violence may be seriously depressed, even suicidal.

Coping with the Violence

Life in a violent household can be oppressive. Since they can't stop the abuse, many young people develop ways to cope with it. They try to make sense of the confusion and, if at all possible, to bring peace to the house.

Many children learn to accept responsibility for things they had nothing to do with. If their parents get fired, have a car accident, or develop a drinking problem, the children blame themselves. After all, they're used to taking the blame for everything else.

Some children cope with the violence by denying that it exists. They tell themselves that there are no problems at home. When someone asks if anything is wrong, they say no. They lie about their bruises and injuries. Denying the abuse makes it easier to get through life. It allows them to separate the things that make sense from the things that don't.

After a while, this mental separation may become permanent. Memories of the abusive events become repressed—locked away in the unconscious mind. Some adults never remember that they were abused as children. Others forget for a time, but their memories return years later.

The Only Life They Know
Young children spend nearly all their time with their families. Until they get old enough to make friends, they know almost nothing about what goes on in other families. For this reason, abused children may not realize that their lives are unusual.

Some abused children remain isolated even when they become teenagers. Their parents may not let them bring friends over or visit other people's homes. As a result, these young people go on thinking that their lives are normal. They believe that all homes are violent places. They accept that being abused is a natural—if unspoken—part of being in a family.

Changing Things Yourself

If you are being abused, you most likely don't want to accept or deny the abuse. You simply want to stop it. You want to make your parents (or other abusive family members) change their behavior.

Unfortunately, as a teenager, there's not much you can do on your own. You still depend on your parents for many things. If you confront them, they may make your life worse than it is already. They may beat you harder, or they may make you feel like a worthless, ungrateful child.

On the other hand, you can't just go out and find another place to live. You've heard how hard it is for teenagers who leave home before they can support themselves. They usually end up on the streets, facing worse problems than they faced at home. In addition, their parents take out their anger on the younger brothers and sisters they've left behind.

This is why you need help. If you live with two parents and only one is abusive, the nonabusive one may be able to help. But many parents in that situation can't or won't do anything. In that case, you need the help of an adult outside the family.

Telling Others

If you are being abused, there are many reasons why you might not want to tell someone about it. You may feel guilty or embarrassed about what you've been going through. You may doubt that anyone will even believe what you say. You may be more comfortable denying the abuse and pretending that it doesn't occur.

The longer you wait to speak up about the abuse, the harder it becomes to talk about it. People who keep such matters to themselves often become isolated and hopeless. They may become depressed and self-hating, sometimes even suicidal. The more they are told that the abuse is their own fault, the more they believe it. And being abused by the people they should trust the most—their parents—makes it difficult for them to trust anyone else.

There's another reason why many young people won't talk about their abuse: they're frightened. They don't know what the consequences will be. They might have to move out of their house. One of their parents might be forced to leave, or even go to jail. Even if a parent has been abusive, the idea of being separated from that parent can be terrifying.

Even when children *want* to tell someone that they're being abused, they may not be able to do so. Their parents may keep them away from other people. Or their parents may threaten them with further violence if they tell.

Some abusers repeatedly promise to change. After each violent attack, they regret what they've done. They apologize and swear it will never happen again. The abused child is likely to accept that promise, especially because it gives him or her an excuse to put off taking action. But promises like these rarely are kept for very long. Soon the child will be abused again and will again face the frightening question of whether or not to ask for help.

Reporting Laws

No one likes to talk about child abuse. Often neighbors, relatives, or friends suspect something is wrong. They see signs that a young person is being abused or that a parent is being excessively violent. But they keep their suspicion to themselves and do nothing about it. They may convince themselves that they're just imagining things. Or they may decide that what goes on behind closed doors is not their business and that they have no right to meddle.

Because it's so hard for people to talk about abuse, every state now has a child abuse reporting law. The laws vary from state to state, but generally they apply to people who have frequent contact with children—people such as teachers, school counselors, child care workers, doctors, and nurses. If these people have evidence that a child is being mistreated, they must report that evidence to the proper authority. (That authority may be the police, a social welfare agency, or a child welfare agency.)

What Educators Look For
Teachers, school counselors, and child care workers are all trained to look for common signs of child abuse. Some of those signs are physical. For example, teachers watch for students

who regularly come to school with bruises, burns, or broken bones. These students may be victims of abuse—especially if they refuse to explain the injuries or if their explanations don't seem believable.

Other physical signs of abuse include odd-shaped bruises, bruises around the head, teeth marks, and bald patches where hair has been pulled out. Students who wear dark glasses indoors, or long sleeves in warm weather, may be doing so to hide signs of abuse.

In addition to the physical signs, abused children often have distinctive ways of acting. Young victims of abuse may shy away from physical contact with adults, or draw back when an adult approaches them. They may show fear when asked about their parents or their home life. They may be hesitant to go home at the end of the day. Some abused children become extremely aggressive. Others become withdrawn.

Neglected children often come to school unwashed, or wearing torn, dirty, or badly fitting clothing. If they are not well fed, they may be underweight or have little energy. With no one paying attention to them at home, they often wear clothes that are inappropriate for the weather. Many come to school with untreated medical or dental problems.

What Medical Personnel Look For
Abused children tend to spend a lot of time in hospitals—especially in hospital emergency rooms. For this reason, doctors and other health care workers are in a good position to watch for cases of abuse and neglect. Even when a parent lies about a child's injuries—which many do—a doctor can often see through the lies.

Willis was beating his son Andrew one afternoon, but he stopped when Andrew stopped screaming. Only then did Willis realize how badly he had hurt his son. He rushed Andrew to the hospital. Andrew had bruises all over his body and a broken arm. When the emergency room doctor asked

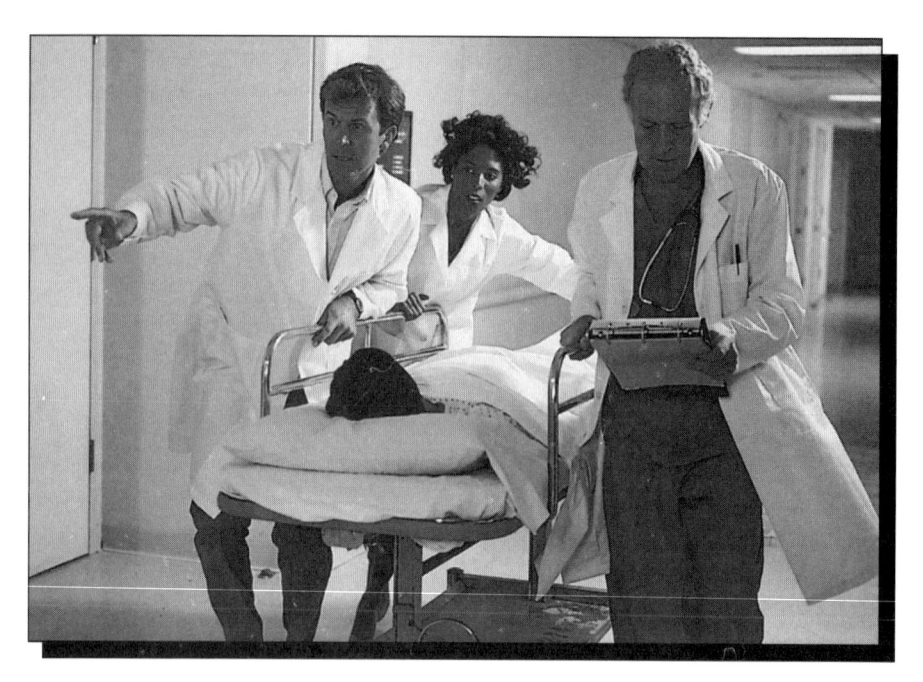

A teenager injured in a beating by his father is on the way to the hospital emergency room.

what had happened, Willis made up a story. He said that Andrew had fallen after climbing onto the roof to retrieve a ball.

The doctor examined Andrew and took X rays. He could tell that Andrew hadn't hurt himself in a fall. The X rays showed that the arm had been broken by twisting. They also revealed three other breaks in Andrew's arm, all of which appeared to have occurred within the last six months. The doctor asked Willis about the earlier breaks. Willis was surprised and unprepared for the questions. He quickly told a story about a series of rollerblade accidents. The doctor, doubting Willis's story, reported the case to child welfare authorities.

When injured children come into a hospital, doctors look for a history of broken bones. They examine burns to see if they were made by cigarettes. They look closely at bruises and cuts to see if the "accidents" really were accidental.

Besides examining the injuries, medical personnel check hospital records to see whether a child has suffered many other accidents. When they listen to the parents' explanation of their child's injuries, they watch for signs that the parents may be lying. Even when parents try to hide what goes on in the home, an alert doctor can find out the truth.

What You Can Do for Others

Even if you are not being abused, you can help end the abuse that others are going through. If you think a friend might be a victim of abuse, try talking to him or her about it. Your friend may find the abuse difficult to talk about, especially if it's sexual abuse. But talking to you will probably be easier than talking to an adult. Once the problem is out in the open, you can encourage your friend to talk to an adult next.

When your friend talks, listen. Don't blame or criticize your friend—remember, the abuse is not your friend's fault. Give him or her whatever information you can, such as books or pamphlets on child abuse. (You can get pamphlets from the school counselor, a local hot line, or any of the organizations listed in the back of this book.) If your friend is afraid to take the books home, offer to keep them at your house.

Persuade your friend to tell an adult about what's going on. Offer to role-play, with you playing the part of the adult listening to your friend. Or offer to go with the friend when he or she reports the abuse.

If your friend still refuses to tell anyone, then you have to—even if you've been sworn to secrecy. You'll hurt your friend more by keeping the secret than by revealing it.

Remember, child abuse is not simply a family matter. Parents have many rights, but abusing their children is certainly not one of them.

CHAPTER 6

What Happens When You Tell

Q My father gets pretty angry sometimes and hits me and my mom. The last time he did it, I almost called the police. But I didn't, because I'm scared of what they would do. What would happen to Dad if I turned him in? What would happen to me and Mom? Who would support us? Would Dad go to jail?

A It's natural for you to be afraid of taking such a big step. At least with the way things are, you know what to expect. You can predict that your father will go on abusing you and your mother. But you can't predict what will happen if you report his behavior to the authorities.

• • • • • • • • • • • •

If you call the police, they will send people out to investigate. They will talk with you and your parents, visit your family at home, and learn as much as they can about the situation. If they think you're in immediate danger, they may separate you and your father temporarily. This will make sure your father doesn't try to "get back at you" while the investigation goes on. He will probably be allowed to keep his job and continue to support your family. There's very little chance that he'd have to go to jail.

You'll be separated from your father for as long as you need to be. As soon as it's safe to do so, the authorities will let him return home. Your family can go back to living without restrictions—and without violence.

How to Tell Someone

We can't say it too often: If you are a victim of abuse or neglect, you need to contact someone who can help you as soon as possible. Your best bet is to call a local child welfare hot line. Look in the phone book for numbers listed under "child welfare" or "child protective services." If there are no such listings, look for the number of a local government health or social services office.

If you can't find a local number, call one of the national offices listed in the back of this book. Tell them where you live, and someone there can give you the number you need. You can also phone or visit the local police or a nearby hospital and ask for help.

You may feel uneasy about talking to someone you don't know. If so, start with an adult you feel comfortable with—perhaps a relative, a neighbor, a teacher, or a counselor at school. That person can then put you in touch with people who can protect you.

Don't Be Afraid
There is no reason to be embarrassed when you talk about what has been happening to you. The people who work in child welfare offices have heard stories like yours before, and they understand what you are going through. They won't blame you—they know you haven't done anything wrong. They also know that reporting abuse is a very difficult thing for a young person to do.

The social workers you talk to will be able to answer all of your questions. More important, they can help make your life better. They want you to have a happy home. It's their job to make sure that no one hurts young people.

What Happens When Abuse Is Reported

Police and social service agencies receive reports of child abuse every day. These reports are made by doctors, teachers, friends, and relatives of children, or the victims themselves.

When a report comes in, social workers or other professionals trained in child welfare issues are sent to investigate the situation. The investigators have three important goals: First, they want to find out what's going on; second, they want to make things better without disrupting the family any more than necessary; third, they want to be as sensitive as possible to the victim's needs and feelings throughout the investigation.

Taking Immediate Action

The first thing the investigators must do is protect everyone from getting hurt. When you make a report (or when someone makes a report concerning you), the investigators check to see if you're in immediate danger. If so, they'll act quickly to separate you from your abuser. If the abuser lives with you, they'll arrange for one of you to move out of the house—at least for a while. If the abuser does not live with you, the investigators may get a court order that requires him or her to stay away from you. Anyone who violates such an order can be sent to jail.

The Investigation

Once everyone is safe, investigators will begin by talking with you and your parents. They may also talk to your neighbors, doctors, and teachers about the situation.

The investigators will check whether there have been any previous reports about the person who is accused of abusing you. They'll meet with him or her to ask questions. They'll pay close attention to the answers, especially if those answers change from one meeting to the next.

In addition to interviewing everyone who may possibly be involved, the investigators may also make surprise visits to your home. They'll want to see for themselves what your family life is like.

Talking to an Investigator
You are the most important person for the investigators to speak with. The investigators know that abuse is difficult to talk about. They'll try to make the conversation as easy for you as possible, but they do need to hear the whole story.

An abused person should not be afraid to tell a complete and accurate story to an investigator.

When you speak with an investigator, it's important that you be as complete and honest as you can. There's no need to hide anything. There's no need to embellish anything to make the story sound worse. Whatever is going on is serious enough.

If you don't know the answer to a question, say "I don't know." Don't try to guess what the investigators want to hear.

If you have trouble talking about the abuse, the investigators may decide to meet with you a number of different times. Telling your story in small pieces may be easier than talking about it all at once. When investigators talk with very young children, they may use props such as dolls or games to help the children describe what happened.

Assessment and Decision

After completing their investigation, the investigators can work out a solution for the problem. The best solution is one that will keep you safe, yet not expose you to the stress of being separated from the people you love. Such an ideal solution is not always possible, but the investigators will recommend what seems best for you and your family.

Treatment and Counseling
The solution to problems of family violence usually includes psychological counseling. Counseling can help abusers learn healthy ways to handle their anger and frustration. It can also help them to deal with underlying problems, such as substance abuse or job stress, that are contributing to their anger. Some abusers want to participate in stress-management classes in addition to one-on-one counseling.

Much child abuse and neglect stems from ignorance and behavior by parents who just don't know how to raise children. For this reason, many abusers are asked to take parenting classes. These classes teach parents how to raise children and how to discipline them without violence.

Abusers who have drug or alcohol problems may be directed to such self-help groups as Alcoholics Anonymous or Narcotics Anonymous. In these groups, substance abusers help each other get over their addictions. At regular meetings, they talk about their personal problems and offer support for each other.

A similar group, called Parents Anonymous, is designed specifically for parents who abuse their children or are afraid that they might. There are Parents Anonymous groups all over the United States.

Abusers are not the only ones who need to be counseled. As a victim of abuse, you might also benefit from counseling. Even if you are no longer in physical danger, you may still have emotional problems because of what happened. Counseling can help you overcome those problems and feel good about yourself again.

Family Counseling
Family counseling—in which the whole family meets regularly

with a counselor—is especially valuable in cases of family violence. Meetings with the counselor might take place once a week or more, depending on what is most helpful. To watch how your family life is changing, the counselor may ask to meet with you in your home rather than in an office. In the case of an abuser living away from the home, he or she would also come for the family sessions.

Abusers are rarely forced to leave home forever. After a period of treatment and counseling, child welfare workers will look again at your family's situation. If the counseling seems to have had a good effect, they'll recommend that the abuser rejoin the family. Assuming no further incidents of abuse occur, the family can continue to live together permanently.

Taking Further Steps

Child welfare workers are not law enforcement officers. They can't force anyone to do anything. They can recommend that the abuser move out or participate in a counseling program. But if the abuser refuses to follow those recommendations—or if the counseling doesn't work—you may continue to be in danger. In that case, the child welfare workers will talk to a judge from the family court or juvenile court. The judge has the power to order that further steps be taken.

The Court System
If the abuser is someone outside of the family, a judge can issue an order requiring that person to stay away from you. This order may be called a peace bond, a protective order, or a restraining order. It usually requires that the abuser keep a certain distance away from you and avoid other kinds of contact with you (for example, by phone or by mail). If the abuser does not comply with the order, he or she can be arrested and jailed.

The judge's role is more difficult when the abuser is a parent or other member of your family. No one likes to divide a fami-

If necessary, when no relatives are available, during the investigation you may be placed temporarily in a juvenile facility. You will get support there from other young people who are experiencing similar situations.

ly for any length of time. Before a judge will permit you and your parents to be separated, he or she will first conduct a careful review. The judge will talk with the investigators about their findings and ask what they recommend. He or she may also ask for the advice of other people, such as social workers, educators, psychologists, law enforcement officers, and specialists in children's legal issues.

The judge will also want to talk with you. This is your opportunity to say what you would like to happen. Your wishes in this matter carry a lot of weight.

Placement
If only one parent is abusive, you may be able to stay with the other parent. If that's not possible, you may be put into the custody of a relative. If necessary, the judge will issue a court

order that requires the abuser to stay away from you. (The abuser may be allowed to see you under special circumstances, such as supervised visits.)

If there's some reason why you can't live at home, the judge may place you in a foster family, group home, or residential juvenile facility. (In a group home or juvenile facility, you would live with other young people who are going through similar situations.) You'll keep going to school and participating in all your normal activities. Your family will still be permitted to visit you and will continue to support you financially.

Young people are put in residential facilities or foster homes only when it's absolutely necessary, and only for as long as it's necessary. The judge who places you will make sure that a social worker reviews your situation regularly. As soon as it's safe for you to be reunited with your family, you will be.

Although it does occasionally happen, it's extremely rare for a judge to order a permanent separation of a child and a parent. That is done only when every other solution has been attempted and has failed. The judge is required by law to do what is best for the child, and permanent separation is almost never the best solution.

What Happens to the Abuser

With counseling and treatment most abusers can learn to change their behavior. It's very rare that an abuser will be sent to jail, especially after the first report of abuse. Judges understand that going to jail rarely helps an abuser and may harm the family.

However, child abuse and sexual abuse are crimes. A judge may order the arrest of an abuser who continues to endanger you or others, refuses counseling, or does not comply with the judge's orders. If the abuser still shows no willingness to change, he or she may be put on trial and may have to serve time in prison.

Interview

When Regina turned 30, she found herself with two small children and an abusive husband. He was abusing not only her, but the children as well. She would have left her husband much sooner than she did, but since she'd never been out on her own, she felt as if she had few options. While no one's story is typical, Regina's experience presents a good idea of what it's like to live with violence.

We met in high school. We started dating when he was in college, and I got pregnant. He was my first love, it was the first time I'd ever had sex, and I got pregnant. So we had to get married—certainly abortion was out of the question. You just did what everyone expected you to do.

Even though my mom and dad were supportive, I know they were disappointed. I was to have this great art career, and now I was pregnant.

So we were married, and I had a daughter. I think I grew to love my husband. I wrote a letter to my mother at one time, singing his praises. I really wanted my family to think I'd done the right thing. I don't know if I was shielding them in some way from thinking I had been forced into something that I didn't want.

And not until the second child was born—by this time we had moved to Michigan—did things start to change. He started seeing a lot of other women.

This man had become very, very angry. He would look at me and get angry because I was innocent, because I had trusted him. So here was this woman looking at him with all this trust that he was not worthy of, and what could he do but be angry? I understand that now.

His father was a holy terror—he yelled at everyone, all the time. I'm sure my husband learned that from his father—this was what he knew—this was how he was taught to behave.

I used to leave notes, "If I'm found dead, he did it." I was certainly terrified. There were outbursts and things being thrown. We all walked on eggshells. This was not a man who drank or did drugs, but he was a rage-aholic. You just did what he said. He had a military aspect to him: "Everybody better mind me; I'm calling the shots here."

He would hit the children in the head, and of course I would have a fit about that. It wasn't as if the children and I huddled in the corner any time he was home, but we were really afraid of him.

There was emotional abuse as well. His sense of humor was really sick. When my son would go out to play—he was only about six—he would come back in and sit down at the table, and my husband would ask him, had he gotten into any little girl's pants? I mean, it was really sickening.

My daughter was hard of hearing, so she had a speech impediment. He has always thought that she was less than perfect. He never really had much to do with her.

And she's had a really hard time with that.

If I knew then what I know now, none of that would ever have happened, but women were raised to keep their mouths shut, no matter what.

I guess it just went downhill from there. A few years later, we moved to California. By this time, this was a very violent and angry man. It was the frustration, I guess. He just didn't like his life. He didn't like himself at work, didn't like himself at home, didn't like himself, period.

It escalated in California. We were separated during the summer—I took the kids to my parents' home in Texas while he moved us to California, where I'm sure he had a grand old time. I met somebody during that time. He was a family friend. Nothing ever came of it, but there certainly was a reawakening in me—I learned there *is* a life beyond all this violence.

I took total responsibility at that time for what was going on around me and realized that *I* had to make my life work for me. I couldn't depend on him to do it, nor was I going to be a victim.

I started reading all the self-help and psychology books I could find. I was looking for reasons to leave as fast as I possibly could. By the time the children and I got to California, it was all over within a year. He'd been very angry, hitting more, being meaner, and he was a terror at work. He became so unbelievably bad at that point that they finally fired him.

I had tons of girlfriends, and I wore them out talking to them about this. Their response was, "Well, maybe you ought to leave." Where would I go? Well, of course, they couldn't help me, and of course, they had their own fears about their own marriages. They were supportive—you always had someone to talk to—but there were never any solutions.

If it were now, I would be out of that marriage in ten minutes. But the fear of raising two children on my own and being told I couldn't do it—that fear kept me in the marriage. We were married for 15 years. That's about 10 years too long.

The children and I had a great life after the divorce. I was earning money that we could spend any way we wanted to. I remember with my first paycheck, I bought a roast, and we sat in front of the oven and through the window we watched it cook. We had a lot of fun. It was wonderful not having that violence in the house. It wasn't roasts every night, but it was happy.

But today, my son has no self-esteem. He never finished high school. He got into marijuana; I think that's the only thing he got into, but I'm not sure. He still isn't doing what he wants to do in life. My daughter is very overweight and is very emotional; she needs counseling. They're both, as far as I can tell, not abusive. I look for that to come up. They have no children of their own.

I think my daughter's husband is abusive—I don't think he hits her, but I know he's emotionally abusive. I've told her to tell me if anything is wrong. I tell her,

"This is abusive, sweetie. Don't just swallow it." She says, "But mother, this is my marriage." I just want to throw up. At least she knows I'm there. That's all I can do. She knows she has help if she needs it.

Today, there are more people out there saying, "If this is happening to you, go get help." No one ever said that to me. If a person is being abused, if they do what's right for them, it's going to also be what's right for the children. I firmly believe that. People don't ever have to experience the fear that I felt. They don't have to put up with that—there is someone to talk to out there. Why do women feel responsible? Why do I feel responsible? How could I? I know better now. Yet I do.

I probably will never marry again. I can't imagine having anybody ever tell me again to come to bed, turn out the light, go to sleep, and shut up.

There's still stuff I'm learning, but I'm sure happy. I have an incredible circle of friends, I am having the time of my life, and I'm really, really happy. Doing it my way.

CHAPTER 7

Righting the Wrongs

Q My name is Sheila. My stepfather abused my brother and me for two years until Mom finally divorced him. I'm scared. I hear all these horror stories about children who've been abused—that they always abuse their own kids, and that they are mentally screwed up for life. Is this true? Am I doomed? Can I never have children of my own?

A Even if the abuse is over or the abuser is gone, some scars may remain. Most physical scars will heal in time. Without counseling, however, the emotional scars may never go away. Counseling can help you learn how to have a healthy life, despite the rough treatment you've had growing up.

• • • • • • • • • • • •

You sound as if you're doing OK now, but you're right to be concerned about your future. Many adults who were abused as children find that memories of the abuse come back later, even though they thought they were "over it." These memories are most likely to come back when you get married or have kids of your own. But you're certainly not "mentally screwed up for life." In fact, some adults who were abused as children are among the most gentle and loving parents.

It's best to begin to deal with what happened right away. That will make it easier to heal the emotional scars, and you'll feel better about yourself and your future.

The Effects of Abuse

Family violence and abuse can cause a great number of physical problems. Some, such as bruises, cuts, and broken bones, soon heal. Others, such as brain damage or hearing loss, may last forever. Prolonged neglect may cause problems such as malnutrition that require great care to overcome. Abuse can also leave a person with emotional, learning, and behavior problems.

Emotional Problems
When young people are beaten by a family member, they have to make sense of an impossible situation: the abuser loves them, but the abuser is attacking them. Neglected children face a similar contradiction: their parents love them, but their parents are ignoring them. Having to believe two opposite things at the same time often leads to emotional problems. Even when the abuse or neglect stops, the confusion about what happened—and why it happened—often remains.

If you've been living in a violent home, you may experience feelings of depression, fear, anxiety, sadness, or guilt. You're likely to have sleeping or eating problems. If you've been subjected to sexual abuse, these problems may be even greater and your confusion even deeper.

Learning Problems
It's hard to get an education when things are difficult at home. If you're living in fear of being beaten, or if you don't get the care and love you need, you can't easily concentrate on your schoolwork. Your self-esteem may sink so low that you don't make it to school at all. Young people who are hungry or ill—or who are worried about the safety of their younger brothers and sisters—also may miss many days of school.

When the mistreatment finally stops, young people who have been abused may have a great deal of catching up to do.

If they've missed a lot of schoolwork, it may take years for them to catch up. Those who are not prepared to do the necessary work may choose instead to give up on school. A great number of school dropouts are children who were victims of abuse and neglect.

Behavior Problems
Young people in abusive situations often get angry, but they don't know how to handle their anger. Some follow the model of their abusers—they take out their anger through violence. They may torture or abuse animals, or hit other people. They may lash out at adults verbally or physically. Many act up in class. Some become self-destructive. They cut or burn themselves, begin to abuse alcohol or drugs, or develop eating disorders. Some of this behavior may stop when the abuse stops. But many of these habits can be very hard to break.

Young people who are beaten or otherwise abused often have trouble developing social skills. They may not know what kinds of behavior are considered acceptable. Some become antisocial and withdrawn. Others become extremely needy, clinging to anyone who will spend time with them. Some go back and forth between being friendly and being hostile. They end up destroying any friendships they develop.

Many children in abusive homes decide to run away. They figure that the dangers of life on the streets can't be worse than what they're going through at home. Unfortunately, they can't run away from the emotional problems they're carrying. Those problems make the already difficult challenge of surviving on the streets nearly impossible.

The Future

Vera was sexually abused by her mother's boyfriend when she was eight years old. The abuse went on for about nine months until she got the courage to tell her mother what was going on.

Her mother immediately broke up with the man. Neither of them ever saw him again. Vera's mom watched Vera closely to make sure she was doing OK. For a long time, she saw no evidence of problems.

Five years later, when she was 13, Vera met her first boyfriend. As soon as they started dating, she started having nightmares. The nightmares only stopped when she broke up with the boyfriend. The same thing happened with her next boyfriend. Throughout high school and college, Vera couldn't stay in any relationship for more than a few weeks. As soon as a boyfriend showed any sort of affection or wanted to get physical, she found herself becoming physically ill and left him.

The teen years are a difficult time for everyone. You have so many new things to get used to. You develop new responsibilities, new relationships, a new sexual awareness, and lots of new anxieties. There are many pressures on you and a lot of things you're uncertain about. A teenager who has a history of being abused—even if the abuse stopped years ago—can become overwhelmed with the difficulties of adolescence.

Romantic Relationships
It can be very difficult for a teenager who has been abused to develop healthy relationships. People who have not received love at home may have trouble when they seek it from others. Some become overly dependent on those they meet. This can make them open to mistreatment and manipulation.

Others actually seek out abusive partners, believing that they deserve mistreatment. They can't maintain a relationship that doesn't have an element of abuse in it and may go from abuser to abuser, never finding a healthy relationship.

Raising Children
Children of abusive parents often have trouble raising children themselves. It's estimated that most parents who abuse their children suffered abuse themselves when they were young. Their

experiences taught them that the way to control behavior is through physical violence. Even though they remember hating what their parents put them through, they don't know any other way to control their children.

Survivors of sexual abuse often don't want to have children at all. They worry that they'll raise a child who will be abused or who will abuse someone else.

Being an Adult

A violent nature, antisocial behavior, low self-esteem, a lack of education, fear and distrust of others—all of these qualities can lead a person to a difficult future. Statistics show that a large percentage of criminals, especially violent criminals, have a history of being abused as children. The unfortunate truth is that individuals who were abused as children often have trouble becoming healthy, productive adults.

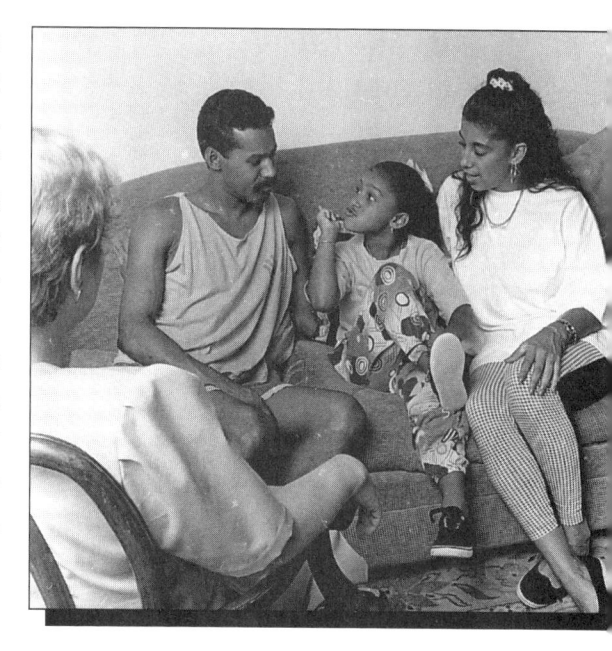

There are many types of counseling available for family violence. Family counseling is a good way for everybody in the family to express his or her point of view and work out a solution together.

Counseling

Fortunately, there is hope for these individuals. If you have been abused, you can get over many of the problems you may have developed. It may take some time and hard work, but it can be done. The most helpful and effective remedy is psychological counseling.

Individual and Group Counseling

Depending on your experiences and your needs, you might choose individual counseling, group counseling, or both. In individual counseling, you and a counselor (a therapist, psychologist, psychiatrist, or other mental health professional) talk alone together. You discuss what happened, how you feel about it, and what would make you feel better. You'll probably get together once a week.

In group counseling, you and a group of others meet together with a counselor. Group counseling gives you a chance to hear others talk about their experiences, which sometimes helps you to understand your own experiences better.

Peer Groups

In addition to more formal counseling, many people find it

Emotional scars may take a long time to heal, but through counseling many families find ways to handle stress, resolve conflicts, and strengthen their relationships.

worthwhile to get together in support groups. This is why groups such as Alcoholics Anonymous and Narcotics Anonymous are so popular for recovering drug abusers. Alateen and Alanon are groups for people who have friends or family members with addiction problems. All of these groups meet frequently in cities and towns throughout the United States. You can find the one nearest you by checking your local phone book.

Working Toward the Future
Counseling can help you come to terms with what you saw and what you experienced. It can help you get over any bad feelings that remain. A counselor can help you understand that you were not responsible for your abuse. And being in counseling gives you a safe place to talk about things. This is important, since not paying attention to your feelings can make you feel worse.

A counselor can help you identify and put a stop to abusive behavior. He or she can teach you how to help others in your family who may also be having troubles. Your counselor can help you overcome your feelings of shame, guilt, and anger. This will help you keep from taking out these feelings on someone else.

Some people are uncomfortable about going to a counselor. They feel that it shows there's something wrong with them. In a way, there is something wrong—you've been mistreated, and that mistreatment may cause you problems in the future. But going into counseling is never something to be ashamed of. It shows that you have the self-confidence to give yourself a strong and bright future.

Where to Go for Help

There are many national organizations that can help you learn more about family violence, neglect, and abuse; several of them are listed below. Each of these places can put you in touch with a counselor or other person who can answer your questions and send you booklets, brochures, and other information about child abuse and family violence.

Your best bet is to get in touch with local organizations. Local groups can get you the help you need right away. To find these groups, look in your telephone book under the words "child abuse," "children's protective services," or "family services." You can also contact a local health center, public health department, social services agency, or the police.

American Association for the
  Protection of Children
63 Inverness Drive E.
Englewood, CO 80112
(303) 695-0811

Childhelp USA
P.O. Box 4175
Woodland Hills, CA 91370
(800) 422-4453

National Coalition Against
  Domestic Violence
P.O. Box 18749
Denver, CO 80218-0749
(303) 839-1852

National Committee for
  Prevention of Child Abuse
332 S. Michigan Ave., Suite 1600
Chicago, IL 60604
(800) 835-2671

National Council on Child
  Abuse and Family Violence
1155 Connecticut Avenue, NW
Washington, DC 20036
(800) 222-2000

Immigrant & Visible Minority
  Women Against Abuse
P.O. Box 3188, Station "C"
Ottawa, ON K1y 4J4
(613) 729-3145

White Ribbon Foundation
#104-220 Yonge St.
Toronto, ON M5B 8H7

Institute for the Prevention of
  Child Abuse (I.P.C.A.)
25 Spadina Rd.
Toronto, ON M5R 2S9
(416) 921-3151

Canadian Society for the
  Prevention of Cruelty to
  Children (SPCC)
336 First St., P.O. Box 700
Midland, ON L4R 4P4
(705) 526-5647

Kids Help Phone
#100 - 2 Bloor St. W.
P.O. Box 513
Toronto, ON M4W 3E2
1-800-668-6868

For More Information

Young Adult Books on Family Violence

Ackerman, Robert J., and Dee Graham. *Too Old to Cry.* TAB Books, 1990.

Berger, Gilda. *Violence and the Family.* Franklin Watts, 1990.

Gilbert, Sara. *Get Help: Solving the Problems in Your Life.* Morrow Junior Books, 1989.

Haskins, James. *The Child Abuse Help Book.* Addison-Wesley, 1982.

Hyde, Margaret O. *Know About Abuse.* Walker and Company, 1992.

Landau, Elaine. *Child Abuse: An American Epidemic.* Julian Messner, 1990.

Mufson, Susan, and Rachel Kranz. *Straight Talk about Child Abuse.* Dell, 1993.

Park, Angela. *Child Abuse.* Aladdin, 1988.

Rench, Janice E. *Family Violence.* Lerner Publications Company, 1992.

Other Books on Family Violence

Finklehor, David. *Child Sexual Abuse.* The Free Press, 1987.

Kurland, Morton L. *Coping with Family Violence.* Rosen, 1990.

Pizzey, Erin. *Scream Quietly or the Neighbors Will Hear.* Penguin, 1977.

Statman, Jan Berliner. *The Battered Woman's Survival Guide.* Taylor, 1990.

Brochures and Pamphlets on Family Violence

"A Look at Child Sexual Abuse." National Committee for Prevention of Child Abuse, 1986.

For More Information

"Emotional Maltreatment of Children." National Committee for Prevention of Child Abuse, 1992.

"Facts about Child Abuse and Neglect." National Council on Child Abuse and Family Violence, no date.

"Facts about Domestic Violence." National Council on Child Abuse and Family Violence, no date.

"Physical Child Abuse." National Committee for Prevention of Child Abuse, 1992.

INDEX

Abuse. *See also* Child abuse; Physical abuse; Sexual abuse
  causes of, 30–33, 35
  cycle of, 26–27, 71–73
  of disabled children, 36
  effects of, 19–20, 47, 51–52, 69–73
  of the elderly, 11, 26
  forms of, 19–25
  future for victims of, 71–73
  nonphysical, 38
  predictors of, 34
  reporting, 57–63
  sibling, 24, 40
  of spouses, 11, 24–25, 34, 40, 41
  ways of dealing with, 49–50
Abusers
  abused people seeking out, 72
  confronting, 46
  court authority over, 61–63
  excuses made by sexual, 41, 43
  profile of, 29–30
  reporting, 57–63
  treatment for, 60–61
Accidents, 23, 54
Alanon, 75
Alateen, 75
Alcohol consumption, 13–14, 31–32. *See also* Substance abuse
Alcoholics Anonymous, 60, 75

Behavior problems of abused children, 71

Child abuse. *See also* Abuse; Physical abuse; Sexual abuse
  effects of, 12, 19–20, 47, 51, 69–73
  facts about, 10, 42
  future for victims of, 71–73
  neglect as, 22
  by parents, 6–9, 20–23, 33, 48
  signs of, 52–55

Child abuse reporting laws, 52
Communicating
  about physical abuse, 12–14, 16–18, 51–52
  about sexual abuse, 45–47
  how to start, 57
  your decision, 16–18
Counseling
  for abusers, 60
  benefits of, 75
  family, 60–61
  for victims of abuse, 47, 60, 69, 73–74
Courts, and abuse cases, 61–63
Criminals, as former abuse victims, 73

Decisions
  communicating your, 16–18
  making your, 14–16
  sticking to your, 18
Disabled children, abuse of, 36
Discipline
  compared to abuse, 12
  methods of, 22–23
  teaching appropriate, 60
Drug abuse. *See* Substance abuse

Elderly abuse, 11, 26
Emotional abuse, 19–22, 33
Emotional needs
  of children, 22
  of families, 33, 35
Exhibitionism, 38

Families, 33, 35, 40–41, 50. *See also* Parents
Family counseling, 60–61
Foster homes, 63
Frustration, as cause of violence, 30–31

Group counseling, 74
Group homes, 63

Hot lines, 4–5, 15
Humiliation, as form of abuse, 21

Immaturity, as cause of violence, 32–33
Incest, 38. *See also* Sexual abuse
Investigations into charges of abuse, 58–60

Marital rape, 40

Narcotics Anonymous, 60, 75
Neglect
 as abuse, 22
 causes of, 35–36
 problems due to, 70
 signs of, 53

Parents. *See also* Families
 emotional abuse by, 20–22, 33
 as formerly abused children, 72–73
 lack of experience in young, 32–33
 neglectful, 35–36
 physical abuse by, 6–9, 48–55
 placement with nonabusive, 62
 sexual abuse by, 38, 40, 41, 43–44, 46, 47
 support systems for, 33, 35, 60, 61
Parents Anonymous, 60
Peer groups, 74–75
Physical abuse. *See also* Abuse; Child abuse; Sexual abuse
 alcohol consumption and, 13–14
 coping with, 49–50
 getting help for, 50–51
 helping others who are experiencing, 55
 laws concerning reporting of, 52–55
 by parents, 6–9, 48–55
 signs of, 52–55
 understanding, 48–49

Placement, 62–63
Police, 56–57

Rape, 40, 41
Running away, 71

Self-esteem, low, as cause of violence, 31, 70
Sexual abuse. *See also* Abuse; Child abuse; Physical abuse
 communicating about, 45–47
 compared to physical contact, 37–38
 effects of, 47
 facts about, 11
 forms of, 38, 39
 reaction of mothers to, 44–45
 reasons for, 40–41, 43
 survivors of, 73
 ways to accomplish, 43–44
Siblings
 abuse by, 24, 40
 helping abused, 35–36
Spouse abuse
 behavior indicating likelihood for, 34
 explanation of, 24–25
 facts about, 11
 rape as form of, 40, 41
Stress, as cause of violence, 30–31
Substance abuse
 as cause of violence, 13–14, 31–32
 groups dealing with, 60
 by individuals who had been sexually abused, 47

Verbal abuse, 21

Witnesses
 to abuse, 21
 mothers as, 24–25